Rex Conway's
STEAM ALBUM

SUTTON PUBLISHING

First published in 2007 by
Sutton Publishing, an imprint of NPI Media Group
Cirencester Road · Chalford · Stroud · Gloucestershire · GL6 8PE

Reprinted 2007

British Library Cataloguing in Publication Data
A catalogue record for this book is available from the British Library.

ISBN 978-0-7509-4626-1

GWR Dean 4–4–0 3545 at Symonds Yat in the Forest of Dean coupled to what looks like an inspection saloon, 1920s.

Typeset in Palatino.
Typesetting and origination by
Sutton Publishing.
Printed and bound in England.

Contents

2–8–0 heavy freight loco No. 3830 returning to South Wales with a train of empty coal trucks passing through Patchway under clear signals.

Introduction

I have written this book in the hope that it will attract those who have a mild interest in railways, as well as the enthusiast who wants to see good photographs of steam locomotives. It is not intended as a reference book for those who want to know every detail, every date, time and minute a certain locomotive passed point X. Although that information is essential to dedicated followers, it can be a bit dry for those who like looking at pictures and reading anecdotes and general information.

Enthusiasts will know all about how the steam locomotive works, and how it is coaled and watered. However, you'd have to be in your fifties to remember the 100ft-high coaling towers, and the water columns at the ends of all platforms. So this book I hope will kindle interest in those of lesser years, as well as appealing to the mature like myself who just want to pick up a book and revive memories of days out on platforms looking at real trains.

I was a professional photographer all my working life and my hobby was railways, so the two came together and resulted in thousands of photographs. Unless I wanted to send a print to one of the railway magazines, I rarely printed them. The negative was more important to me so I amassed a large collection.

In recent years I have had several collections of negatives donated to me by older people who wanted a good home for their treasures. I have also bought collections and now have an archive in excess of 60,000, although like any collector, be it of stamps, teapots or whatever, I am always looking to acquire more.

All the photographs in this book are from my archive. Regrettably, quite a few have no information or sometimes misleading information. I have tried to make sure of facts but I do not know every location or date so I am sure someone will spot a fault and let me know. I have included a small selection for which I have no detail at all; if you can supply any information it will be appreciated. Please contact me via the publisher.

A young author winding his camera on after taking a picture of No. 4970 *Sketty Hall* on a stopping train at Highbridge, summer 1949.

Rex Conway's Steam Album

Once upon a time there was a baby boy born within 500yd of Bristol's main station – Temple Meads. He didn't know much about it at the time but Temple Meads would be a Mecca for him for a long time. That little boy was me, and the year was 1937 – 14 February to be precise. I was a Valentine baby and my love for the steam engine was born at almost the same time, as by the age of 3 I am told I used to spend hours in the top bedroom of our three-storey home, watching the trains going in and out of the east end of Temple Meads. Then Mr Hitler intervened. Severe bomb damage to our house and the area persuaded my parents that life expectancy in our house could be short, so my mother and I and a number of cousins went to live for a short while in Senghenydd in South Wales. It only had a small station at the end of a branch line, but if I disappeared the family knew where to find me: where else but the station?

The next four years were spent travelling round the southern half of Britain with my father who was in the RAF. I saw exotic locations such as Newquay, Bournemouth and Cambridge, to name but a few. Travel was always by rail, keeping my interest alive. One memory I have is of St David's in Pembrokeshire in 1943. The nearest station was Haverfordwest and the remainder of the journey was by bus. The road journey was past one of the many beaches in the area. It was when the bus was trying to get up the hill past the beach that the passengers had to get out and push it to the top. The war ended and by 1946 we were back in Bristol. By this time I was old enough to go to Temple Meads by myself to experience the excitement of the railways, of seeing hundreds of passengers thronging the platforms going to all parts of the country.

An aerial view of Bristol Temple Meads. I was born in a house by the river (top right). All the houses had been demolished when this photograph was taken.

Senghenydd, where I spent a few months away from the bombs falling on Bristol. In the background are the remains of a coal mine that closed after a tragic accident in the early twentieth century.

Passengers leave 'The Bristolian' at Temple Meads with No. 6000 *King George V* at the head in June 1954.

Ian Allen train-spotting books were available to encourage the enthusiast and the railways were still operated by the 'Big Four' companies, with the GWR's locos being most in evidence at Temple Meads. Although many of the locomotives were dirty and rundown, a 10-year-old boy hardly noticed when locos with names like *Knight of the Grand Cross* and *Skylark* came steaming through. The LMS also used part of the station. I remember various 'Jubilees', and once a very unusual visitor, *Royal Inniskilling Fusilier*, brought a train in from the north.

'Star' class No. 4018 *Knight of the Grand Cross*, one of my earliest memories.

Another of my childhood memories: GWR No. 3454 *Skylark*.

A visit from a 'Royal Scot', in this instance No. 46120 *Royal Inniskilling Fusilier*, which came to Bristol, early 1950s.

By the age of eleven we moved to a more rural part of Bristol and a new school, which by coincidence was only a few hundred yards from Fishponds station on the main LMS line out of Bristol to the north with local trains to Bath. The school dinner hour was 12 till 1 and the 'Devonian' was due through the station during this time, so it would be no surprise to find a number of schoolboys on the platform waiting to see it. The line from Temple Meads was up quite an incline and levelled off just past Fishponds. The first view of the express with its headboard was an unforgettable sight. A plume of smoke and steam and the roar as the train swept through the station made school worthwhile.

'The Devonian' headboard,
Bradford–Paignton.

No. 44534 arriving at Fishponds with a stopping train from Gloucester.

The 'Devonian' from Bradford to Torquay and Paignton was nearly always hauled by a 'Jubilee'. Bristol had a number of these locomotives – No. 45561 *Saskatchewan*, No. 45572 *Eire*, No. 45577 *Bengal*, No. 45660 *Rooke*, No. 45662 *Kempenfelt*, No. 45663 *Jervis*, No. 45682 *Trafalgar*, No. 45685 *Barfleur*, No. 45690 *Leander* and No. 45699 *Galatea*. Most of these had spent their lives based in Bristol in order to work the northbound express.

No. 45660 *Rooke* awaiting its next duty at Barrow Road.

No. 45577 *Bengal* passing Nibley on its way north.

No. 45663 *Jervis* about to depart from Sheffield southbound for its Bristol home.

No. 45686 *Barfleur* on the southbound 'Devonian' approaching Mangotsfield on the outskirts of Bristol. This line has disappeared and is now the Bristol ring road.

It was while at this school that my interest in railway photography was kindled. My parents had friends in the London area and on several occasions my father and I went to Euston station. Of course I used to tell my train-spotting school friends about the engines I saw on these visits, and was always greeted with derisory comments accusing me of telling porkies.

On one visit to London I borrowed my father's box brownie and took a roll of eight exposures. My efforts were very poor but the locomotives' numbers could be read. I realised then that photographing these giants was the way forward. By 1950 I had made several trips to London using a slightly better camera with improved results. The next step was to build an enlarger with the help of my father and try to do bigger prints than the small contact prints. My early experiments with a home-made enlarger were not wonderful and stretched my pocket money because of the high wastage. However, I kept trying and eventually I produced passable prints, even having several pictures produced in railway magazines.

On leaving school I got a job on the local newspaper as a copy boy in the editorial department. I had only been in this department for a short while when a vacancy arose in the photographic department for a trainee printer. In other words, sweeping the floors, making up chemicals, etc., but I learnt the trade. At the same time I was adding to my railway photographic collection. There were visits to the local sheds, in particular Barrow Road (22A), where a long road bridge crossed the yard. The coaling tower was to one side and the shed on the other, so all the action could be seen from this vantage point.

Sunday morning was the best time, especially in the summer when all the locos that had worked specials down on the Saturday would be stored at the side of the shed. After viewing and photographing everything from the road bridge it was round to another small road bridge that had a commanding view of these locos and the back of the depot. A fairly low wall separated the enthusiasts from the simmering locos, so there was a well-worn path from the wall to our favourite subjects.

A quick up and down of the lines collecting numbers and taking photographs was a regular Sunday occurrence until one day a mean-minded foreman – or at least that was our view – had the top of the wall coated in dirty waste grease. Not that young determined train-spotters were beaten by such an act – a couple of thick potato sacks soon overcame that man-made obstacle.

Barrow Road shed, with Class 5 No. 45042 over the ashpit. This photograph was taken from the road bridge.

Another view from the road bridge looking towards the shed, with two of the Bristol 'Jubilees' on view: No. 45690 *Leander* and No. 45682 *Trafalgar*.

A selection of locomotives photographed from the wall that was covered in grease.

Unfortunately when I was away from home in the RAF, my mother, wanting my room to be nice and tidy when I came home on leave, threw out all my notebooks with records of my sightings and dates of photographs, so I have to rely on memory for my early spottings.

One of these memories is of going to Fishponds station one lunchtime to be greeted with the sight of No. 45516 *The Bedfordshire and Hertfordshire Regiment*, a 10B Preston engine at that time, parked on one of the sidings. On enquiring of the driver, we were told he had worked a pigeon special down from the north to Mangotsfield. Just up from Fishponds, the pigeons – thousands of them – were released and then raced back north. Another rare sight at Fishponds on three evenings in either 1951 or 1952 was 'Royal Scot' No. 46113 *Cameronian*, which had come down from the north. I never found out why. It must have been a trial run to see if 'Royal Scots' were suited to the Bristol line. Whatever the reason, it was not until the early 1960s that we saw regular 'Scots' in the area. It was while I was still a spotty adolescent that I made several trips to the north, Manchester, Liverpool and other cities. In the early 1950s, to me, steam engines seemed to be nose to tail in these areas. I only had enough film to take about 100 exposures so I had to ration the views I took. Regrettably I probably missed many rare subjects as my concentration in those days was on the big engines which were never seen in my part of the country: A4s, 'Duchesses' and the like.

Many hours were spent at Temple Meads which was not the easiest station in which to find the perfect photography spot. The Midland engines left from the old Brunel station at the east end, while the GWR sheds at Bath Road were at the west end. Fortunately the refreshment rooms were halfway down the platform, so frequent visits were made for lemonade and delicious fruit pies. From the end of the platform a fine view could be had of the sheds with a constant coming and going of mainly passenger locos: 'Kings', 'Castles' and 'Halls'. There were a few tank engines that were used as station pilots.

Opposite ....

Top: 'Patriot' class No. 45516 *The Bedfordshire and Hertfordshire Regiment*.

Bottom: Class 5 No. 44812 passing the carriage sidings at Mangotsfield where the pigeons were released.

Below: Bath Road shed, Bristol, 1950s. This view was taken from the end of the platform.

One of my favourite locations for taking photographs was Patchway on the northern outskirts of Bristol, where Rolls-Royce had an engine development plant. Not that it was of much interest to a 16-year-old railway enthusiast. That is, until a sunny day in 1953 when two police cars disgorged a posse of policemen and surrounded me. It took quite an explanation but they finally believed I was not a Russian agent covertly photographing Rolls-Royce. The reason I was under suspicion was that the test beds for the jet engines backed right up to the railway line. There was me making sure I didn't get all the chimneys and buildings in my picture, while the security guards of Rolls-Royce thought I was trying to get them in, so they alerted the police.

No. 2841, one of the Churchward 2–8–0 heavy freight locos, nearing the top of Patchway Bank.

No. 6019 *King Henry V* with the Up 'Red Dragon' passing the jet-engine test plant at Patchway.

Patchway station with No. 5062 *Earl of Shaftesbury* passing through.

I went on learning my trade in the darkroom. I was even allowed out on occasions with a camera, which stood me in good stead when the brown envelope with OHMS on the outside arrived and I received a polite request from The Queen to join her forces. After a few months of pleasant guidance from those nice RAF drill instructors, I was selected to become a photographer – something of a novelty, as I discovered when I arrived at the RAF school of photography in Wellesbourne Mountford near Stratford-upon-Avon. There were about thirty on the course and only a few of us had any photographic experience.

My time in the service was on Lancasters and Shackletons, which themselves have become favourites at air shows. On release from the RAF I became a photographer on the Bristol Group of Newspapers, which meant I had much better equipment and cheaper film. Regrettably I had less time, although I still managed to enlarge my collection of railway negatives. I visited my old haunts of Patchway, Nibley and many others. I made many trips to London, visiting all the main stations and sheds. My favourite route on arrival at Paddington was a quick dash down the stairs on to the tube to King's Cross, half an hour or so there, then to St Pancras for a similar period there, then to Euston, where at the arrival platforms there would always be a couple of named locos. Then I'd buy a ticket for Willesden, and get a quick view of the departures, where usually a 'Duchess' could be seen at the head of a service for Scotland. The local train from Euston to Willesden passed the sheds at Camden, so a photograph of these was a must from the train window. A visit to Willesden shed always produced a variety of engines, as it handled passenger and freight locomotives.

Old Oak Common was only just down the road from Willesden. By now it was time to start on the homeward journey back to Euston and Paddington, and to collapse on the carriage seat worn out, but knowing I had a nice lot of fresh negatives.

On one of these trips at King's Cross station a London enthusiast said he could show me how to get into King's Cross shed. Having applied for permits to visit the top shed and been refused, this was an opportunity not to be missed. I am very hazy about the location of the way in, but it was in the vicinity of the gasholders, that well-known landmark between King's Cross and St Pancras. I remember it was a stable. We climbed a ladder through a hayloft and came out on to tracks that led to the shed. We must have looked like scarecrows, with hay sticking out of our hair and clothes, but it was worth it for the sight of gleaming A4s, A3s and others. We managed to see and photograph most of the locos in the yard, although discretion was needed near the offices. For some reason shed masters seemed to get a little cross on spying young people wandering on their territory. Now in mature years you can see how dangerous it was, but youth never sees the danger.

After passing through the Doric arch at Euston, the arrival platform was the first to be reached. Here No. 46143 *The South Staffordshire Regiment* has just brought in a Manchester train.

King's Cross shed with A4 *Wild Swan* ready for duty.

Willesden Junction with No. 46238 *City of Carlisle* at speed hauling 'The Caledonian' near its destination of Euston after its long journey from Scotland.

During the late fifties the main-line diesels started to appear. With them came the realisation that steam was living on borrowed time, so I started travelling more, taking as many photographs in different places as I could. I had bought an Austin Mini and travelled many hundreds of miles in it. I would go off sometimes for a week, sleeping in the car. I must have been far more supple than I am now. My memory of parking in lay-bys, waking in the mornings, and frying sausages and bacon on a small Primus stove still makes my mouth water just thinking about it. By now I was a regular contributor to the various railway magazines.

The family Mini in which I travelled many miles pursuing steam engines.

Opposite ....

This photograph of No. 63932 south of Grantham was taken at 5.45 a.m. after a night in the car and a breakfast of sausages and bacon, June 1962.

I was not very keen on diesel. My interest waned. I had by then taken some 15,000 negatives. In 1962 I got married and in December 1963 our first daughter was born, so spare time was in short supply and railways were put on hold for a few years, especially as steam had all but gone from the West Country by 1964.

The final days of steam in 1968 took place in the north, far removed from Bristol, so I took no part in the final fling, but I did obtain negatives of some of the many special runs that took place to mark the passing of an era. After 1968 steam was banned from even working specials. Various preservation societies were formed.

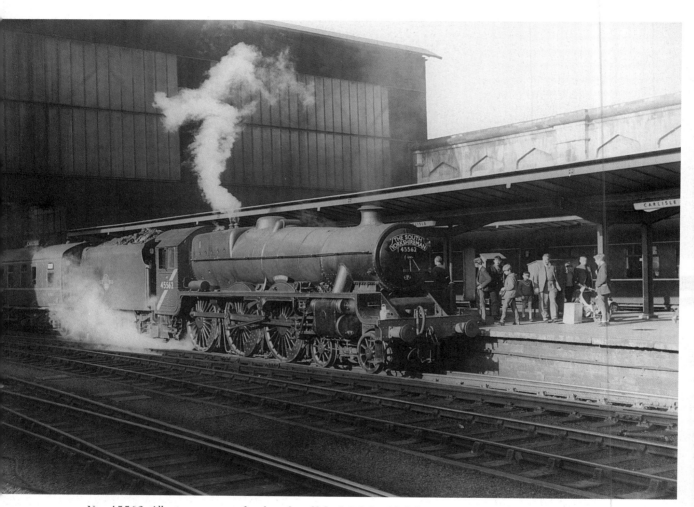

No. 45562 *Alberta* was one of only a handful of 'Jubilees' left by the mid-1960s. This photograph was taken at Carlisle.

Opposite ....

Top: A Locomotive Club special using T9 No. 120, now preserved, Reading.

Bottom: Another special, this time at Birmingham Snow Hill, with Southern Railway 'Battle of Britain' No. 34064 *Fighter Command*.

A large number of steam engines were bought by Woodhams of Barry for scrapping. As luck would have it, Woodhams had also bought a great number of trucks to be broken up and they started cutting these up first. Many societies and individuals started to buy the rusting giants for preservation. The sale of these locos was so successful that all but a few were saved.

One of the saddest sights any railway enthusiast can see. A breaker's yard, this one in Newport, South Wales, with Southern Region U class 2–6–0 31625 waiting its fate.

A pile of locomotives reduced to bits at Cashmores scrapyard, Newport.

This picture shows how big steam engines are. Here I am sitting on the chimney of No. 6024 in Woodham's Yard, Barry.

This was the reason I climbed up on No. 6024: to obtain a picture showing how many locomotives were in Barry.

Now beautifully preserved and in running order, No. 71000 *Duke of Gloucester* looks a sorry sight in Barry minus many parts, including its cylinders.

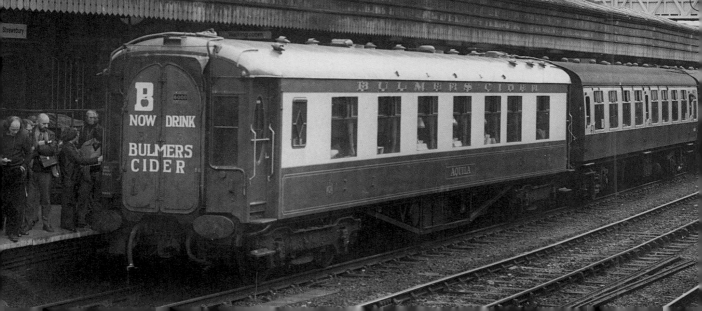

Above: An historic occasion in Swindon, as *King George V* is hauled from a shed into the open by members of the public. On the buffer beam is the Mayor of Swindon. The locomotive then went for an overhaul before going on to Hereford.

Left: Bulmer's Pullman coach at Newport.

H.P. Bulmers of Hereford had private sidings and a rake of Pullman coaches. Peter Prior, the managing director of Bulmers, wanted a steam engine to stand with these Pullmans. GWR No. 6000 *King George V* had been preserved by British Rail as part of the national collection. In turn it was leased to Swindon Corporation and kept in a shed at Swindon. Swindon Corporation agreed to lease the engine to Bulmers, providing it was kept in good order. So the 6000 Locomotive Association was set up in Hereford to look after the superb engine.

Steam locos were still banned from the main line, but in 1971 Peter Prior persuaded BR to allow *King George V* to haul the Bulmer rake of Pullmans on a special train. I knew nothing about all these arrangements. As a professional photographer working for a newspaper my work took me almost anywhere. On that day in 1971 my assignment was to a little place called Severn Beach about 15 miles from Bristol, although the beach can be difficult to find. But for a railway enthusiast not interested in a beach, its main attraction was its proximity to the east entrance to the Severn Tunnel, that gigantic Victorian achievement of more than 4 miles beneath the estuary. I found out just before leaving the office that the special train was due through the tunnel shortly after I had finished work. The gods were smiling. It was a beautiful day so I decided to try for a picture of the train leaving the tunnel. The photograph I took of *King George V* was used by many magazines and newspapers both in this country and abroad. It was this photograph that involved me with the 6000 Locomotive Association. Eventually I became editor of the society magazine and a committee member.

I think it can be fairly said that Peter Prior and Bernard Staite of the 6000 Locomotive Association did more than most to get steam back on the main line, but one also has to praise the volunteers of all the preservation societies, especially the many friends I made at Hereford who worked long hours in all weathers to keep the 'King' in pristine condition. I did feel guilty on many occasions as all I did was take photographs after they had finished their hard work.

The first main-line run with *King George V* was so successful that many more were to follow and continue to this day. Bulmers Railway Centre for a while became home to No. 6201 *Princess Elizabeth* and No. 35028 *Clan Line*, and many other giants of the steam world were visitors.

This picture of No. 6000
King George V leaving the Severn
Tunnel revived my interest in
railways and set me on the road to
Hereford.

Peter Prior and Bernard Staite at
Bulmer's Hereford Railway Centre.

Visiting loco at an open day at Hereford: *Flying Scotsman* attracts the crowds.

Three giants of Hereford: *King George V*, No. 6201 *Princess Elizabeth* and No. 35028 *Clan Line*.

One of the many steam specials that were run over the Newport–Shrewsbury line. This is No. 6201 *Princess Elizabeth* heading south near Ludlow.

Nearing the top of Llanfihangel Bank, *Flying Scotsman* and *King George V* with the Bulmers' Pullman cars.

Another special for enthusiasts: No. 7808 *Cookham Manor* and No. 5900 *Hinderton Hall* nearing Stratford-upon-Avon.

Another major event that took place in the steam world was the 150th anniversary celebrations of the opening of the Stockton to Darlington railway. The celebrations and cavalcade took place in Shildon, not far from Darlington. The 6000 Locomotive Association was invited to take *King George V* but because of clearance problems at certain stations in the north it was decided not to take the loco. H.P. Bulmers, together with the 6000 Locomotive Association, had a display and sales area and I contributed photographs for display. The only parts of *King George V* that made it to Shildon were the bell and the name-plate. It was a wonderful sight . . . engines on view ranged from tiny veterans to the last locomotive built for British Rail, No. 92220 *Evening Star*. They were parked inside a huge shed and in the yard, and finally paraded past thousands of people. The weather on the final day was perfect blue sky and sunshine. I was one of the privileged few who stayed on site and saw all these locomotives in the dawn when volunteers brought them to life, from the first wisps of smoke from the chimneys in the early morning light to the jets of steam from the pressure valves in brilliant sunshine. I doubt if the atmosphere of that week in 1975 will ever be repeated.

The 6000 Locomotive Association display and sales area at Shildon.

The indoor display of steam.

Dawn has not long broken in this view from a lighting tower.

Sir Nigel Gresley being positioned for the Grand Parade.

Getting ready for the off; all the locomotives are lined up and the Grand Parade is about to start in glorious sunshine.

The replica of *Locomotion* shows what the trains of 150 years before would have looked like.

Hardwicke, one of the locomotives that took place in the races to Scotland in the 1880s and 1890s.

No. 92220 *Evening Star*. This was the last steam locomotive built by British Railways at its Swindon Works in 1961.

Caledonian Railway 0–4–4T
No. 419, built in 1907, withdrawn
in 1962.

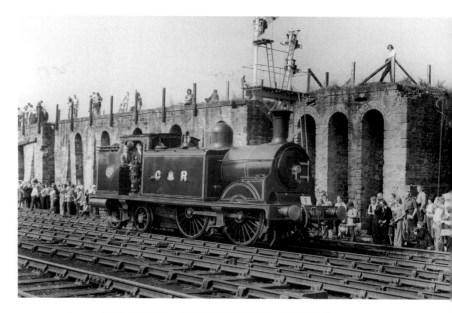

Southern Region 'Merchant Navy'
No. 35028 *Clan Line*, one of the
most powerful locomotives in the
cavalcade.

One of the smallest locomotives in
the parade, Wantage Tramway
Company No. 5.

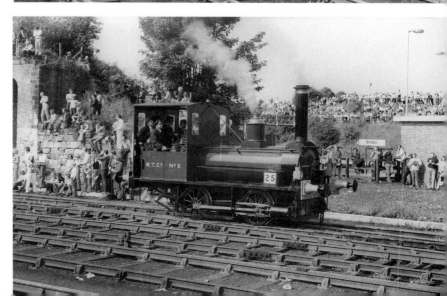

Although I am mainly a GWR enthusiast, the 'Jubilee' class of the LMS takes some beating for appearance, especially No. 5690 *Leander*, which spent most of its life shedded in Bristol.

Sir Nigel Gresley and Great Northern Railway Stirling No. 1 passing Shildon signal-box.

My archive of negatives was growing steadily and by the mid-1990s numbered approximately 60,000, dating from the early 1900s to the end of steam, including about 1,500 views of various stations. On looking at some of the country stations one can only wonder if Dr Beeching had feelings, allowing with the stroke of a pen the destruction of such wonderful buildings. Athough the railways started with freight, passenger traffic quickly followed. And when you have a travelling public, you have to have somewhere they can buy their tickets and shelter from the rain, so the station came into being and many that were built at the start of the railways lasted until the Beeching cuts. Then many were bulldozed to the ground and lost forever. Some escaped but were so-called 'modernised'. There are not many stations left in their original form.

Some platforms were so small that they were called halts. Some halts were used on special occasions and usually built near a racecourse or football ground. At country stations the stationmaster may have only had a lad and a signalman to help him, but he kept his station immaculate. There were flowerbeds, even roses round the doors, and there was always a cheery word for his passengers. The large terminuses were far too busy for such niceties. The stationmaster would have hundreds of staff and be far too involved to be seen on the platform except to receive or see off important people. Porters would help you with your baggage, at a price. And if you didn't have the price you staggered from platform to bus wishing you hadn't brought the kitchen sink with you.

Llandecwyn Halt, not far from Porthmadog, mid-Wales.

Above: Much Wenlock, near Ironbridge in Shropshire.

Left: Wilton, near Salisbury, looking almost brand new in this view of No. 3021 picking up passengers.

....

Opposite

Top: Maryport, on the Maryport and Carlisle Railway. The locomotive is 2–4–0 No. R1.

Bottom: Ashley Hill station, Bristol, *c.* 1900. This was later enlarged to four tracks and has now reverted to two tracks. The young spotters on the grass are possibly from the nearby Muller's orphanage, now converted to flats, which fans of the TV programme *Casualty* will know is where the outdoor scenes of the hospital are filmed.

On the British railway system there are hundreds of bridges. Some are plain, and some defy gravity, such as the arches over the Thames at Maidenhead designed by Brunel and scoffed at by his critics who said they would fall down as soon as the supports were removed. His critics were silenced and the bridge is still there, with HSTs thundering over it more than 150 years later.

The Royal Albert Bridge spanning the Tamar between Saltash in Cornwall and Plymouth in Devon is another masterpiece by Brunel. It's a suspension bridge with a difference. The rail level is suspended from a huge tube which was assembled on the banks of the river, then floated to the site on barges. The construction was then jacked into position inch by inch on to supports more than 100ft above river level. All this back in the 1850s with what modern engineers would call primitive equipment. The equipment may have been primitive, but with a genius like Brunel, who could almost certainly have taught modern engineers a thing or two, it was just another project.

Another bridge that defies belief by us mere mortals is that over the Forth, in Scotland. With thousands of tons of steel like some giant Meccano construction, how could anyone have worked out where all the bits went? And yet it's been there well over 100 years, defying all the gales and extreme weather the Firth of Forth could throw at it.

Another great builder was Robert Stephenson, and his Britannia rail bridge over the Menai Straits connecting North Wales with Anglesey completes the rail and sea route to Ireland. The bridge was opened in 1850 and its crowning glory was the entrance guarded by two huge lions, yet another tribute to the pride the Victorian engineers had in their designs. They wanted them to look good as well as stand the test of time.

A4 No. 60004 *William Whitelaw* has just crossed the Forth Bridge and is passing through Dalmeny station.

This view of No. 60160 *Auld Reekie* clearly shows the complexity of the girder work that forms the Forth Bridge.

A fine view of the Royal Albert Bridge between Plymouth and Saltash, taken from the carriage window.

The Britannia Bridge over the Menai Strait connecting North Wales and Angelsey has something of an Egyptian look about it.

Delving into my archive I came across this negative of policemen standing in front of Agecroft shed. I am reliably informed that the picture was probably taken in 1926, the year of the General Strike. The railways became a target for some of the more militant strikers and police guards were put on all major installations, sheds, stations, etc. There were ugly scenes between strikers and those who tried to continue to run something of a rail service.

The long arm of the law at Agecroft, near Manchester, during the General Strike of 1926.

Signals on the early railway systems were very primitive, almost an afterthought. Among the first signals was what can only be described as a contraption that was controlled by a railway policeman. It could be likened to what we occasionally see on the roads where a workman stands with a pole with a circular board on top, one side reading 'Go', the other side 'Stop'. On the railway there were no words, just a circle and bar meaning the same things.

A great many varieties of signals were tried but eventually the semaphore was accepted on all railways. On the LMS the board or peg, as the signals were commonly called, went up when the track ahead was clear and stayed level for danger. On the GWR the signal board was lowered for clear. The LNER was similar, and the Southern followed the LMS. All these signals were controlled by wires from signal-boxes. I don't know why they should be called boxes because they were built with typical railway care, in many cases being very ornate, and the signalmen who manned them had great pride in keeping them immaculate, with levers highly polished. You would never see a signalman handling his levers without a polishing cloth in his hand. You could almost see your face in the lino on the floor.

The signals were operated on what is known as a block system. One signal-box controlled a block of track. This could be a few hundred yards at busy sections like stations or miles in quiet countryside. A system of bells was used. Signalman A would ring four beats of the bell which were repeated in the box of signalman B to let him know he had an express in his block and would signalman B accept it? If B accepted he would return four bells to A and the train would have a clear path, and so it would go on. From box to box, from Penzance to the north of Scotland, different bell codes were used for different types of trains.

GWR signals at Taunton.

Straddling the tracks at Chester is No. 6 signal-box.

Signal-box at Todderstaffe, near Blackpool, with an LNWR Claughton passing the box, 1920.

Rural signal-box, Shepton Mallet, Charlton Road, in Somerset, early twentieth century.

Canwick signal-box on the Great Northern Railway, clearly showing the somersault signals.

The interior of St John's signal-box on the Isle of Wight.

The Victorians were master builders and made sure buildings were appealing to the eye. And the same was true of lighting. By today's standards the illumination they gave was poor. This was before the use of electricity, so gas was the main fuel for station and shed lighting. But what the lighting installations lacked in quality of light was certainly made up for in quality of design. Each railway company had its own lamps, often with its initials incorporated. The lamps were usually copper or brass and were often highly polished. When electricity came along most of the gaslights were converted, ensuring that they lasted until the modernisation scheme when they were thrown away by the thousand and replaced with efficient but totally austere lights. Pictured here are a few examples from various early railways.

Among the thousands of negatives I have collected over the years are several views of small locomotives on a beach. There are no records stating where the photographs were taken. It was suggested to me that it might be Blackpool. This prompted me to write to a Blackpool newspaper, which kindly printed one of the photographs together with a letter from me appealing for information. The response could not have been better. A letter arrived from Brian Turner who lives in Lytham. He had made a study of this event that took place in 1911 in Blackpool and was locally known as the 'Sands Express'. Brian had written a detailed article in 1968 and he has given me permission to use it, although this is a shortened version.

The Blackpool borough engineer James Brodie was responsible for widening the promenade between the North and Victoria piers in 1905, and in 1910 work began on extending the promenade from North Pier to Cocker Street. Brodie's plan was to build a concrete wall 500yd long on the beach and then fill the space between this and the old sea wall with sand. To be precise, some 226,000 tons of it. Owing to various sea defence improvements, a change in tide patterns had caused vast amounts of sand to be deposited at the southern end of the town, almost reaching the top of the sea wall. It was estimated that a strip of the beach roughly 50yd wide from St Chad's Terrace in the north to just south of Victoria Pier would produce the amount of sand required for the new promenade. In 1910 this was no problem. Just lay a railway track to transport the sand along the seafront. Try doing it nowadays with all the rules and regulations that govern us! There would have to be public meetings to hear objections. In Bristol, where I live, a ring road was built for all but a couple of miles. This final 2 miles took a further ten years to complete because several gentlemen objected to a cycle track having to be diverted. Thousands of local residents wanted the ring road completed but the few held it up for all those years. I always thought democracy meant the vote went to the majority. So Mr Brodie was lucky it was the Victorian era when things like common sense were used.

The railway was built in January 1911 between the tramway and the sea wall, with the rails and sleepers laid directly on the asphalt surface. Two locomotives and forty wagons were hired. The engines were *Netherton* and *Horbury* and they arrived in February and were immediately put to work. The sand was loaded at Victoria Pier by a gang of eight men with shovels. Work was speeded up with the addition of more tracks and three more locomotives, *Reliance*, *Annie* and *Alice*, and by 18 May 1911 the vast amount of sand had been shifted and work came to an end. This was much to the relief of many residents, as the use of poor-quality coal for the locomotives had meant black smoke drifting through the town.

Opposite ....

Top: The 'Sands Express' being loaded at the south end of Blackpool's beach, with *Annie* and *Alice* simmering in the sun.

Bottom: With a full load of sand, the two engines work hard to get up the steep incline to the level road surface.

As a photographer of the steam locomotive I would always try to shoot moving trains at a spot where the engine would be working hard, with smoke coming out of the chimney and giving an atmospheric picture of the type loved by enthusiasts everywhere. As a lover of the steam engine I can, however, see they are not very eco-friendly, and one would have thought designers like Churchward, Stanier, Gresley and the like could have produced locomotives that did not smoke. Here are a few pictures of excessive smoke, which was frowned upon by most railway employees as it was usually caused by poor-quality coal or poor-quality firing. Most enginemen prided themselves on a clean exhaust. On most railway lines in suburbia, houses backed onto the railway. Washing days must have been a nightmare for the housewife. Clean washing quickly got covered in smuts. Perhaps they should have changed the traditional washday of Monday to Sunday when traffic was lighter.

One can only imagine what the whites on this washing line, only a few yards from the main Midland line out of Bristol and the coaling tower at Barrow Road shed, will look like when they are taken in.

4–6–2 Class A2 No. 60539 *Bronzino* leaving Hartlepool.

Midland Railway 2P No. 708 shows very well the effects of a dirty fire.

Another dirty fire at the head of the pre-war 'Flying Scotsman'. The offending A4 is No. 2510, as yet unnamed.

Southern Railway Mogul
No. 31822 also darkens the sky.

Another Southern Railway
locomotive making an action
photograph is 'Battle of Britain'
No. 34089 *602 Squadron*.

'Fowler' 4MT 2–6–4T
No. 42301 passing Tebay in a
cloud of smoke.

Somebody who knows all about bad coal and brick arches is Ron Prince, who was a fireman driver during the 1950s and 1960s. The brick arch, an essential part of heating the water and creating steam on a locomotive, was often the cause of engine failure. On the lovely warm evening of 30 June 1962 the efforts of the crew of No. 45735 *Comet* on the relief 'Mancunian Express' were put to the test just north of Bletchley when the arch collapsed on to the fire, which had the effect of taking the heat out of the fire and a consequent loss of steam.

With the train travelling at speeds in excess of 80mph the footplate was not a steady platform. However, under these conditions the crew managed to get the bricks out of the firebox by using fire irons and a shovel, piled them up on the metal part of the footplate, cooled them down with water then threw them out of the engine.

From then on it was the skill of the driver and Ron Prince working together that maintained time. They still managed 90mph, and Manchester was reached on schedule. As with all faults that developed, a repair card was filled out by driver Jack Burton and when the fitters examined the locomotive they could not believe that the crew had reached Manchester, let alone on time.

Headboard of 'The Mancunian', Euston–Manchester.

The inside of a firebox, showing the brick arch.

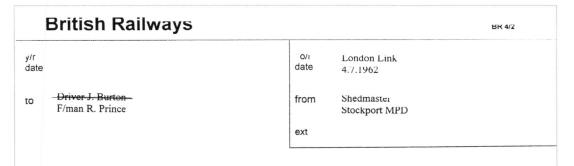

British Railways

BR 4/2

y/r date		o/t date	London Link 4.7.1962
to	~~Driver J. Burton~~ F/man R. Prince	from	Shedmaster Stockport MPD
		ext	

5/50 RELIEF LONDON EUSTON-MANCHESTER L.RD 30.6.1962
LOCOMOTIVE 45735

It has been brought to my notice that whilst you were in charge of the locomotive working the above express, it suffered a partly collapsed brick arch passing Bletchley.

I would like to thank you for your efforts on arriving in Manchester on time without requesting a fresh locomotive en route. Well done.

Ian Lockwood,

Acting Shedmaster

The letter that Ron Prince received from a grateful shedmaster.

In pouring rain No. 46115 *Scots Guardsman* backs down on to 'The Mancunian' at Euston.

Opposite

Top: Rebuilt 'Jubilee' No. 45735 *Comet* approaching Crewe.

Bottom: Another view of *Comet* passing Tamworth with an express.

Brick arches were especially vulnerable when the locomotive was working at full power, especially on steep banks. It's a bit like driving a car up a steep hill in low gear with your foot pushing the accelerator to the floor. The effect on a steam engine is to create a terrific blast in the firebox at the point where the brick arch takes most of the force.

Banking engines spend most of their days going uphill under full power and freewheeling back down. The Americans call them pushers. They were stationed at the bottom of steep inclines to help heavy trains to the top. One of the steepest gradients on the British network was the Lickey Incline on the Bristol–Birmingham route at Bromsgrove. At 1 in 37 it was considered very steep, although a car driver would not even notice it. But then a car was unlikely to have 300 or 400 tons hanging on the back of it. The LMS built a very powerful engine to help trains to the top of the Lickey. It had a number of nicknames but the most popular was 'Big Bertha'. It was a 0–10–0 but by the 1950s it was worn out and was replaced by as many as four small engines to do the same work.

Another incline which was a nightmare for engine crews was from the Severn Tunnel to Patchway. It wasn't as steep as the Lickey but was much longer and also included the Severn Tunnel and Patchway Tunnel, where the banking crew had the exhaust of the train engine as well as their own to cope with. Imagine the scene: tunnel walls only a few feet from the side of the cab, sulphurous smoke, hot steam, the red glow from the fire, the crew with wet cloths over their faces. This was not a job for the faint-hearted.

No. 6166, one of the Severn Tunnel Prairie tanks (so called because of its 2–6–2 wheel arrangement), nears the top of Patchway Bank.

'Big Bertha', the 0–10–0 Lickey banker, pushing a northbound express through Bromsgrove.

Western Region 2–6–2T No. 5156 is seen here having just left Patchway Tunnel.

Another skill the fireman had to learn was the use of the water scoop. The steam engine is a very thirsty piece of machinery and needs constant refills, so much so that it would probably only travel 40 or 50 miles before the fireman started getting jittery and tapping the gauges. The problem was overcome by the use of water troughs enabling trains to be run long distances without stopping. It seemed a simple solution. The fireman on the engine lowered a scoop into a trough full of water, and the tender was filled with water in a minute or so. Sounds simple, but there is nearly always a 'but', as a fireman will relate. Ron Prince recalls one incident he was involved in.

After an overnight lodging at Willesden Railwayman's Hostel he booked on at Camden locomotive depot and was told to work the 5.12 p.m. Blackpool relief train from Euston. The rostered engine was No. 45643 *Rodney*, a 'Jubilee' class loco. Driver Jack Moores and Ron worked *Rodney* light engine back to Euston where they coupled up to twelve coaches. They were booked to stop at Rugby, Nuneaton and Stafford, and also Crewe where another crew would take the train on to Blackpool. Ron's instructions were to take water at five different troughs on the journey. His most memorable one was Hademore. *Rodney* did not have its normal tender. It was fitted with a Fowler tender and the water gauge wasn't working. Hademore was a difficult trough to work as there was a level-crossing just before it and the scoop had to be lowered as soon as the road was crossed. Too soon and the scoop broke, leaving a nice big gouge in the road and no water in the tender. *Rodney* was travelling at speed when Ron lowered the scoop. He had lowered the scoop perfectly and water was rushing into the tender. But with the gauge not working it was guesswork as to when sufficient water had been taken. And this is where Ron lost the smile on his face. He was a few seconds too late in bringing the scoop up and hundreds of gallons of water poured onto the footplate soaking the crew. Ron had to fire the engine with his trousers drying in front of the fire. *Rodney* ran into Stafford with Ron trying to hide his embarrassing lack of apparel from everyone on the platform.

Ron Prince.

Class 5 No. 45280 shows clearly the effects of not getting the water scoop up quickly enough.

'Jubilee' class No. 45643 *Rodney* at Birmingham New Street.

The water scoop under the tender of *King George V*.

A pre-war view of 2P No. 452 with inspection coach at Brock Troughs, north of Preston. Judging by the direction of the smoke, it was travelling backwards, suggesting an inspection was taking place.

The first-coach passengers must have got wet on this train, headed by Eastern Region Class B1 No. 61051.

No. 6200 *Princess Royal* at speed on water troughs.

Apart from water troughs, every station had facilities for supplying the water a steam engine needed, where in a very short time, thousands of gallons could be pumped into the tender. Situated at the ends of the platforms were water columns, each with a long leather pipe. The driver had to bring his loco to a halt opposite the column and the leather pipe was inserted into the filler on the tender or tank. This was a team effort as the fireman climbed up on to the tender while the driver swung the pipe over and operated the valve which started the flow of water. Each column had a coal brazier with a long funnel which kept the water flowing in freezing weather.

GWR No. 16 *Brunel* at Oxford, 1902. This view shows the water column and the way two problems were solved; a gaslight gave illumination at night and the heat from the light stopped the water freezing in the pipe in frosty weather.

Pannier tank No. 9615 has just been given a drink at Westbury.

A London & North Western Railway water column at the end of Stoke station.

My archive contains thousands of negatives from the early 1900s to the 1980s. Some 15,000 I have taken myself. The collection is now over 60,000. Many have been donated, the early negatives I have bought. I am not a believer in collecting and keeping them hidden away; I would rather share my enthusiasm for the steam engine and early diesels with like-minded collectors, therefore I make them available as I know my photographs bring pleasure to many enthusiasts. I am always interested in obtaining more negatives for the collection so please contact me if you want a good home for your negatives. The following pages are from some of the earliest negatives. I have gathered as much information as I can, but if the reader knows of any inaccuracies I am always pleased to hear from them.

LNWR 4–4–0 'George V' class No. 2663 *George the Fifth*. Station unknown.

Opposite ....

Top: GWR 2–2–2 *Royal Albert* at Oxford, 1901.

Bottom: GWR 'Saint Class' No. 2904 *Lady Godiva* waits for the green light at Teignmouth, Devon.

North Eastern Railway No. 1519, a racy-looking 4–2–2 at an unknown location.

Furness Railway 0–4–0 No. 16A. Little is known about this locomotive. However, the tender is piled with coal so it appears to be still in use at the time the photograph was taken.

Another view at Oxford: No. 102 *La France*, early 1900s.

North British Railway No. 486 at Carlisle, early twentieth century.

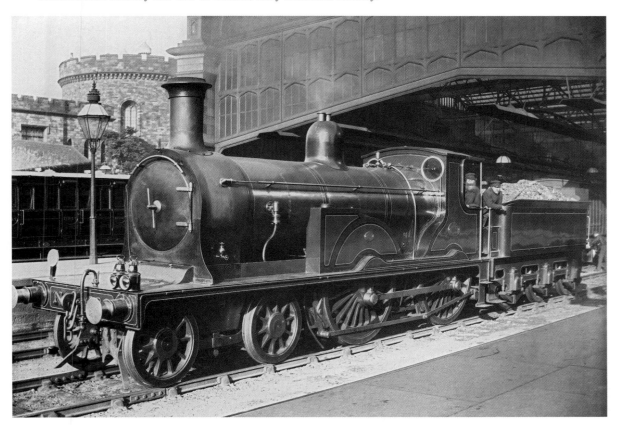

A locomotive that did not survive the Second World War. No. 4911 *Bowden Hall* received a direct hit from a German bomb and was completely wrecked.

A photograph of what is thought to be a quarry engine, early part of the twentieth century.

Proud workmen pose in front of brand-new London & South Western Railway 4-6-2T No. 516, early twentieth century.

GWR crane tank locomotive No. 17 *Cyclops*.

In the 1900s, long before the health and safety rules came in to make life far safer but more boring, engine drivers would frequently take their children to see daddy's engine, or perhaps grandad's. In those days a driver and fireman would be allocated their own engine, which they would make sure the cleaners kept immaculate. Before 1923 and the so-called grouping when all the small railways were grouped into four companies, locomotives were to be seen in colours from bright blue to black, with gleaming brass and polished copper everywhere. There is no denying that it was hard and dirty work keeping an engine clean. But there was a look of pride on the faces of the engine crew when arriving at a station to the admiring looks from the passengers.

Spotless Glasgow & South Western Railway locomotive No. 10 with two young lads in their Sunday best, believed to be at Dumfries shed, 1900s.

Opposite ....

Top: GWR 4–2–2 *Avalanche* with gleaming brasswork.

Bottom: How many hours were spent getting this London & South Western Railway locomotive as spotless as this?

In the early days of railway photography, cameras were quite large and frequently attached to heavy tripods, so the photographer was very evident, with the result that many photographs had the driver, fireman and anyone else who happened to be there posing for the camera. They nearly always had a serious look because if conditions were a bit on the dull side a time exposure of perhaps a second or so had to be given. The photographer would call out 'Keep nice and still' – hence the fixed look.

Cleaners pose in front of London & South Western Railway locomotive No. 425.

Opposite ....

Top, left: Somerset & Dorset Railway crew aboard No. 19.

Top, right: Could the gentleman in the bowler hat on the footplate of Midland Railway No. 4 be the driver or an inspector?

Bottom, left: A North British Railway crew pose for the camera.

Bottom, right: The driver makes last-minute checks on an LBSCR locomotive about to leave Victoria station.

In the 1890s, when the various railway companies were in competition with one another, the London–Edinburgh route was considered to be a natural racetrack, being almost the same distance on the east coast as it was on the west coast. The race to the north was on. It became so aggressive that a halt was called before a serious accident occurred. Things went quiet for many years until the 1930s, when the LNER and the LMS both started building streamlined locomotives. The LMS set a new world speed record for a steam engine when a publicity express from Euston to Crewe reached nearly 114mph, although it nearly came to grief at Crewe when it entered the station at 50mph instead of the permitted 20mph. The record did not last long, however, as we all know that the LNER's *Mallard* achieved the incredible speed of 126mph. Fortunately good sense prevailed once more, and although the LMS and LNER continued to run non-stop to Scotland from King's Cross and Euston, they no longer raced.

Streamlined LMS 'Coronation' class No. 6221 *Queen Elizabeth*.

Opposite ....

Top: Another streamlined 'Coronation', No. 6225 *Duchess of Gloucester*, at Shrewsbury.

Bottom: *Mallard* approaching Bristol Temple Meads on a charter train, 1960s.

Apart from scheduled trains, all the railway companies ran specials mainly to seaside stations for their own staff. After the Second World War the tradition was carried on. Now known as excursion trains, many factories in the industrial north and Midlands would hire complete trains to take their staff to the seaside as a gesture of appreciation for loyal service. It's a shame that loyalty is sometimes not appreciated to the same degree these days. Blackpool was one of the most popular destinations. This is a picture of one of the many excursions from the Manchester area to Blackpool fired by Ron Prince. No. 45709 *Implacable* headed an Oldham's Batteries special from Denton near Manchester to Blackpool, where this publicity picture was taken of the loco crew with some of the ladies from Oldham's.

August, the traditional holiday period, saw special trains to all parts of the country, with the West Country seeing a huge increase in the number of trains running at the weekends, which often led to queuing outside some stations. Bournemouth was also a popular destination, with many trains from the Bradford and Manchester areas leaving the main line to the West Country at the rural setting of Mangotsfield just to the north of Bristol, and taking the Somerset and Dorset line from Bath to Bournemouth.

Some of the happy staff of Oldham's Batteries arrive at Blackpool in the summer of 1962.

Opposite ....

Top: A Saturday special on its way to the seaside headed by Class 5 No. 44856 passing Nibley, near Bristol, 1962.

Bottom: Another Saturday special, this time heading north with 'Royal Scot' class No. 46100 *Royal Scot*, also at Nibley.

Another method of keeping an express non-stop was the slip coach. Generally this was only on long-distance trains like Plymouth to Paddington, although there were fast trains from Bristol to Paddington that slipped a coach at Reading. Passengers could board these expresses even though it didn't stop at their destination. As long as they stayed in the slip coach, which was the last coach on the train, they would arrive at the station they wanted. As the express approached the station where the coach was to be slipped, still at high speed a guard in the slip coach would release the coupling and by use of the handbrake bring the coach to a halt at the platform. Sometimes if the express was on the centre track the coach was stopped short of the station and a shunting engine would propel the coach alongside the platform. Many minutes were saved by this method. When the diesels came on the scene this practice gradually ceased.

A coach being slipped at Reading.

Opposite

Locomotive power was obviously stretched to the limit as WR 2–8–0 No. 5253 heads a special from Weston-super-Mare to South Wales, August bank holiday 1960.

Railways started with freight, not passengers. Many years before railways, coal was moved by horse and cart, then by barges on the canals, until someone had the idea of putting the carts on rails. Compared with today's rails they were very primitive; made of wood they were more like guide rails. Later they were made of cast iron and the wheels ran on top of the rail, as they do now 200 years later. The traction though was still horsepower – an expression we still use.

The freight train spelt the end of the canals for mass transportation of freight, but not before a lot of unpleasant scenes, both political and physical. Freight was carried all over the growing system. South Wales had a branch line in almost every valley where there was a coalmine, all of them leading down to the main lines and dock areas at Barry, Cardiff and Newport. The trucks used would carry the name of the private company that owned them. Other freight areas were the Midlands and Lancashire mill towns, which saw one of the first railways in Britain, the Liverpool to Manchester route, which of course saw *Rocket* hauling freight trains. The First World War saw a huge increase in freight traffic to supply the war effort, as did the Second World War. Then came the motorways and big lorries. The railways started to feel the effects from the competition, as had the canals in the early 1800s. One can't help but feel that the politicians were very short-sighted, although it was probably impossible to predict the congestion on Britain's roads now and the huge costs involved in dealing with today's problems. With the benefit of hindsight we can see that it might have been far cheaper to have kept a lot of the lines and subsidised public transport.

Southern Region Q1 33001 passing through Redhill with a freight train.

Opposite ....

Top: 'Patriot' class No. 45518 *Bradshaw* heads a freight train on SHAP.

Bottom: LMS 3F No. 43263 heads a local freight past Mangotsfield, near Bristol.

No. 47996, one of the big Beyer-Garrett locomotives of the LMS, built especially to work coal trains from Nottingham to London, leaving Elstree tunnel, 1953.

A Western Region local freight at Aller Junction, Devon, headed by Hawksworth 0–6–0 PT 9440.

An early LMS freight locomotive, No. 12488, near Carlisle, 1925.

An unusual visitor to Patchway, No. 9023 was more commonly seen on the Cambrian coast. These locos were built from redundant 'Duke' frames and 'Bulldog' boilers, and nicknamed 'Dukedogs'.

Sheds, or depots as they are called nowadays, were to be found everywhere from Penzance to Thurso and Dover to Holyhead. Some were tiny, home to one or two locos, while the biggest could accommodate nearly 300 engines. Locomotives were allocated to a depot that required that class to work a specific type of train in the area. For instance, a 4–6–2 'Duchess' class loco, which is a powerful passenger engine, would not be allocated to a shed that required freight trains. A 'Duchess' would be found at sheds like 1B, which is Camden, London, for working the heavy expresses out of Euston to Scotland, like 'The Royal Scot', 'The Midday Scot' and 'The Caledonian'.

Freight engines would be allocated where industry required goods to be moved. Many sheds given over almost entirely to this type of engine could be found in the Midlands and the north, though many sheds would have a mix of passenger and freight locomotives, plus a few tank locos for working branch lines. One of the biggest freight sheds was at Toton in the Nottingham area, and this was devoted almost exclusively to working coal trains. Most of the South Wales sheds also had allocations of heavy engines to work coal trains. Among the biggest sheds in Britain were Newton Heath in Manchester, Stratford in London and St Margaret's in Edinburgh.

The larger the shed, the more repair work could be carried out. If a major failure occurred, the locomotive would be sent to a large works. All locomotives also went to works for regular checks. These were done on a mileage basis, much the same as a car has regular maintenance. A heavy overhaul meant the locomotive was virtually stripped down to the last nut and bolt. Sheds were also a service area for visiting engines. A locomotive relieved of its train would go on to the local shed. It would receive coal and water and be serviced. This involved opening the smokebox door and getting all the cinders out that had accumulated, shifting several hundredweight of almost-dust by shovel and brush. The fire had to be cleaned, involving the use of long fire irons to get rid of dead clinker. Ash was dropped into a pit by the use of a rocking system of bars under the fire. All bearings would be checked and oiled. All this work was mainly carried out by shed staff. The driver and fireman would have handed the loco over to the staff and gone to the offices to fill out a report card on the engine to notify any problems. The engine was then left to simmer quietly until its next duty.

Drummond Standard 0–6–0 goods 57392 at Balornock, Scotland.

Opposite

Top: No. 46245 *City of London* at Camden shed.

Bottom: Two Class 5 locomotives at Newton Heath shed.

A high vantage point view of Brighton shed.

Eastern Region B1 No. 61281 in the afternoon sunshine at Peterborough's New England shed.

Reading GWR shed, 1957.

Carmarthen shed, 1930s.

Coaling at sheds varied. Many had 100ft-high towers. A loaded coal truck was hoisted to the top of the tower. Its load was tipped into a huge chute which could be controlled and a measured amount of coal deposited in the tender of a locomotive. Smaller sheds used a mobile crane with a grab that could lift coal into the loco. The Great Western preferred a different method. A building higher than the locomotive was constructed with an inclined track up which laden trucks were shunted. Coal was then loaded into small wheeled bins that were pushed by manpower on to a tracked platform above the locomotive and their loads tipped into the tender.

Another laborious way of filling the tender.

The tender is filled very quickly from this 100ft-high tower.

Opposite ....

A slow way of coaling a locomotive.

The principal locomotive works on the various regions had specialist staff and equipment to deal with all aspects of locomotive maintenance and construction. It seems impossible to me that these works could assemble a vast number of bits and a few days later out would come a complete working steam engine.

The same was true of a heavy overhaul. A very tired engine could be brought in leaking steam and clanking from every loose bearing. It would be stripped completely, with all parts submerged in a cleaning bath, then renewed or renovated, and put back together. It was also repainted and a gleaming, good-as-new loco would roll out. The railway works manufactured everything that was needed to run a railway. Swindon on the Great Western built all forms of rolling stock, including coaches manufactured by highly skilled carpenters and specialist craftsmen. In the early days the works even produced their own gas and later electricity, and had their own hospital and schools. The other regions had similar capability at their factories. All the workers were heavily involved during the war years, making guns, bombs and even small airplanes. Much of this work was of course secret and in the main managed to avoid Hitler's attention.

Wheels at Swindon.

Opposite ....

Top: An 0–6–0 about to move on to the test rollers at Swindon. In the background is 'Pacific' 4–6–2 *The Great Bear* under repair; at that time it was the only 4–6–2 locomotive in Britain.

Bottom: 'West Country' No. 34004 *Yeovil* under repair at Eastleigh.

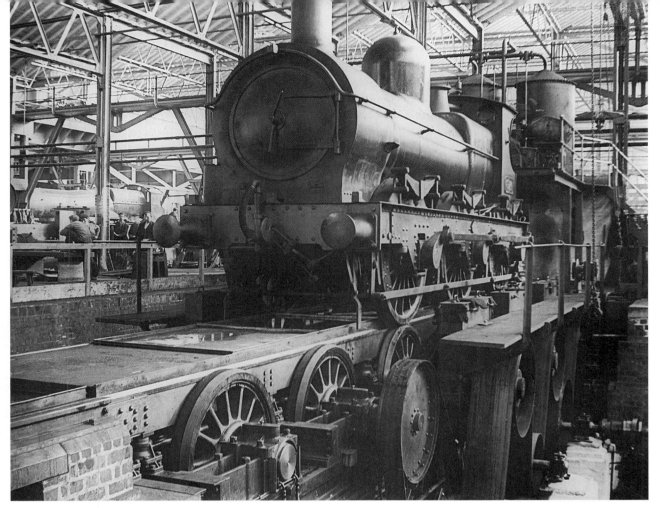

A newly built 'Battle of Britain' class locomotive with continental style numbering at Brighton Works.

Class 5 45092 at Crewe receiving minor repairs. In the background is an austerity locomotive.

An A4 gets a major overhaul at Doncaster.

Wren, a narrow-gauge workhorse, at Horwich works.

Many stations attracted train-spotters and photographers and at the major stations they could be seen in their hundreds.

Crewe, as all spotters and enthusiasts will know, is the junction for a number of main lines to Scotland, Manchester and North Wales. The huge works and shed are at the north end of the station. At the south end the main line heads for London, with diverging lines for Shrewsbury and the Cambrian coast and also South Wales and the West Country. The main line also carried traffic for the Derbyshire, Nottingham and east coast areas, so there was a constant flow of trains, and more than enough to keep notebooks and cameras busy. There were also the spotless engines emerging from the works, shunting engines busying themselves moving carriages around the station, and a steady flow of goods trains, making Crewe a must for those with a keen interest in railways.

No. 46107 *Argyll and Sutherland Highlander* leaving Crewe North shed to back down to the station.

Opposite ....

Top: Class 5 No. 45311 arriving at Crewe from the south.

Centre: A view of the north end with a Standard Class 5, an electric locomotive, 'Jubilee' class No. 45595 *Southern Rhodesia* and 'Royal Scot' No. 46165 *The Ranger* (12th London Regiment).

Bottom: Work-stained streamlined 'Coronation' class No. 46243 *City of Lancaster* leaving Crewe, 1948. The streamlining was removed a few months after this photograph was taken.

Bristol, where the GWR was born, was another very busy station where principally Western Region locomotives could be seen. The Midland also used the station, with trains to and from the north via Gloucester and Birmingham. In later years the occasional Southern and Eastern engines were to be seen, as well as several named trains: 'The Bristolian', 'The Devonian' and 'The Cornishman'. From the west end of the platforms a commanding view could be had of Bath Road shed. As you would expect, this is where hundreds of spotters could be found.

Churchward 2–8–0 3807 with a freight train at Temple Meads.

Opposite

Top: Just arrived at Bristol Temple Meads with the southbound 'The Devonian' is 'Patriot' class No. 45536 *Private W. Wood VC*.

Bottom: No. 4077 *Chepstow Castle* waiting for the off.

Doncaster, another Mecca for enthusiasts, also had a large works near the station. New and reconditioned engines could be seen in great variety. It was also the main route from London's King's Cross to Scotland. Many cross-country routes also passed through the station. Regrettably I did not manage to visit the station until after the steam age, but among my archive are many negatives of Doncaster, including the famous 'Flying Scotsman' express passing through.

Two young train-spotters watch A1 No. 60128 *Bongrace*.

Opposite ....

Top: No. 60073 *St Gatien* makes a smoky start out of the station.

Bottom: No. 60103 *Flying Scotsman* with an express on the centre road on its way through Doncaster.

A Southern Region station I visited frequently was Southampton. Although not a big station, it was busy, being on the main line from Waterloo to the holiday destinations of Bournemouth and Weymouth. It was also on the route from Portsmouth to Bristol and Cardiff. These trains passed through Salisbury, where passengers could change for trains to Devon and Cornwall. Passengers on trains leaving the west end of Southampton would also have a view of the ocean terminals, where the liners berthed.

'West Country' No. 34093 *Saunton* with the famous Southampton clock in the background.

Western Region 'Hall' class No. 4979 *Wootton Hall* on its way to Bristol with a Portsmouth to Cardiff train.

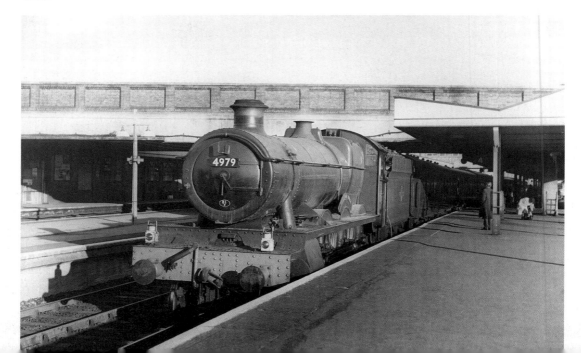

'Merchant Navy' No. 35028 *Clan Line* on its way to Bournemouth.

A view of Southampton Docks from the carriage window.

Glasgow had three principal stations – Central, Queen Street and St Enoch. I have no personal knowledge of these stations as my finances in my teens were very limited and Glasgow was beyond my reach. I feel my education in the railway world left something to be desired. Fortunately there are a great many views of Scotland in my archive.

No. 46239 *City of Chester* starts its long journey south with the 'Caledonian Express' from Glasgow Central.

Opposite ....

Top: LMS No. 14199 at Glasgow St Enoch.

Bottom: The concourse at Glasgow Queen Street.

Shrewsbury was a must for rail enthusiasts until the 1960s. Trains from South Wales and the west of England passed through on their way to the north. Expresses from London to Chester and North Wales included the 'Cambrian Coast Express'. And if that was not enough, Shrewsbury was a running-in destination for new and reconditioned locos from Crewe works, seeing giants like the Stanier 'Duchess' class locomotives on local stopping trains – a far cry from their usual duties of hauling heavy trains between London and Scotland.

GWR 4–4–0 'Bulldog' No. 3701 *Gibraltar*, Shrewsbury Station.

Opposite ....

Top: 'Castle' class No. 7025 *Sudeley Castle* leaving Shrewsbury with a southbound express.

Bottom: LMS 'Royal Scot' No. 46124 *London Scottish* photographed before the roof of Shrewsbury station was removed.

Cardiff, the Welsh capital and principal station in South Wales, had many express services to London and the north, and a train-spotter could also expect to see many coal trains passing through. South Wales had many small railway companies before 1923, which is when the grouping took place, and the GWR took over most of them. The engines of these companies were given new numbers from 1 to 999 and were known to the spotters as the low-number locos. If an enthusiast wanted to see the low numbers, Cardiff was the place to go.

No. 6846 *Ruckley Grange*, an 82B Bristol engine, a frequent visitor to Cardiff on trains from Portsmouth.

Opposite ....

Top: An 0–6–0PT carrying an express headcode passes through Cardiff station.

Bottom: One of the low-number engines, 0–6–2T No. 42, at Cardiff East Dock shed.

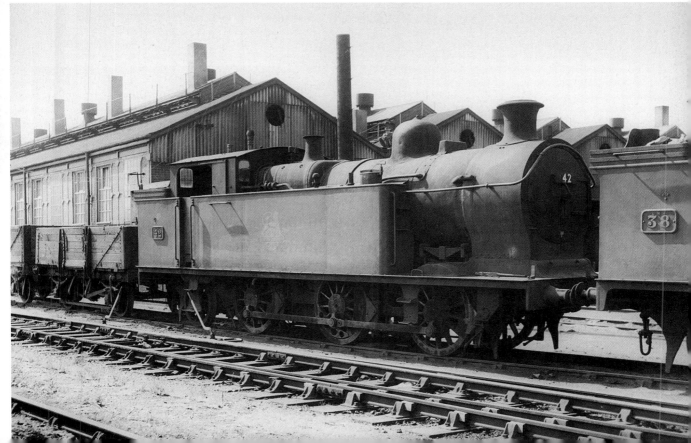

Birmingham had two large stations. If you were a devotee of the LMS you headed for New Street; if you were a fan of the GWR you chose Snow Hill.

No. 40080 on a local stopping train at Birmingham New Street.

One of the last 'Patriots' to be named, No. 45509 *The Derbyshire Yeomanry*, at Birmingham New Street.

'Hall' class No. 6904 *Charfield Hall* approaching Birmingham Snow Hill with a short freight train.

No. 5061 *Earl of Birkenhead* preparing to leave Birmingham Snow Hill.

No. 2833 with another freight approaches Birmingham Snow Hill.

If you were a London spotter or railway photographer the opportunities were almost limitless. Every region had at least two terminuses. The Eastern Region's main terminuses were King's Cross and Liverpool Street. King's Cross served the east coast route to Scotland through many large stations including Doncaster, York and Newcastle. It was also on this line that *Mallard* achieved the world speed record of 126mph. Liverpool Street was the terminus for the east coast route to Cambridge, Norwich and the Fenlands.

Waterloo was the station you departed from if you were holidaying in the West Country and travelling via Salisbury and Yeovil. The 'Atlantic Coast Express' for destinations like Ilfracombe and Padstow left here daily. Bournemouth trains also went from Waterloo. Victoria mainly supplied trains to Brighton and Kent, though passengers travelling to the Continent, in particular France, left on board possibly one of the best-known expresses, 'The Golden Arrow'. Another Southern Region station was Charing Cross. A lot of suburban trains left this station, with some expresses using the North Kent lines.

The LMS main station was Euston, with trains to Scotland on the west coast route, and fast expresses to Birmingham. The many named trains that left here included the 'Emerald Isle Express' with passengers for Ireland.

Paddington was the main departure station for the West Country, with routes to Birmingham, North and South Wales and Bristol. During the 1930s the fastest train in the world, 'The Cheltenham Flyer', arrived at Paddington. St Pancras, situated between King's Cross and Euston, was the terminus for trains from the north via Sheffield, Leicester and Bedford. Nowadays it has been nicknamed 'The Bedpan Line' – not very flattering.

Station pilot at King's cross N2 0–6–2T 69512.

No. 60114 *W.P. Allen* on arrival at King's Cross.

Another arrival at King's Cross, No. 60062 *Minoru*.

An 0–6–0PT No. 4672 on loan from the Western Region, shunting empty stock at Waterloo.

Southern Region No. 751 *Etarre* receives attention to the smokebox door at Waterloo.

A 'Merchant Navy' class locomotive No. 21C19 French Line CGT is admired by a young train-spotter at Waterloo.

'Battle of Britain' No. 34056 *Croydon* ready to leave Waterloo with a west of England express.

2–2–2 *Albany* at Victoria station, early in the 1900s.

No. 34086 *219 Squadron* shortly after leaving Victoria station with 'The Golden Arrow' express.

A 4–6–2T waiting to leave Victoria.

Making sure all the bits are in the right place.

Judging by the horse carriages on the right, this photograph of 0–4–4T *Billingshurst* at Victoria station must have been taken at about the turn of the twentieth century.

The now-preserved No. 46203 *Princess Margaret Rose* preparing to leave Euston station.

Opposite

Top: One of the arrival platforms at Euston station, with 'Patriot' class No. 45529 *Stephenson*.

Bottom: No. 47668 shunting carriages at Euston.

'Castle' No. 7017 *G.J. Churchward* leaving Paddington in the evening sunlight.

No. 1506, one of the heavy shunting engines, at Paddington.

A view of 2–4–0T No. 3589 taking water from the tower that was situated between the lines into Paddington, early 1900s.

Unusual motive power for 'The Royal Duchy'. This service was unusally headed by a 'King' but on this occasion 4704, a heavy freight engine, was used.

'Castle' class No. 5017 *St Donat's Castle* about to leave Paddington, 1930s.

'Jubilee' class No. 5616, before receiving its name-plates, backs out of St Pancras station. In the background are the gas-holders that were a feature of the area.

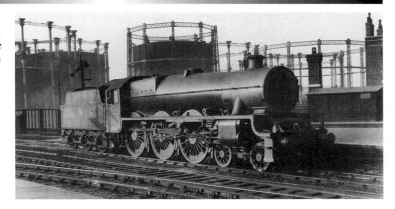

An 0–4–4T shunting stock, St Pancras, 1920s.

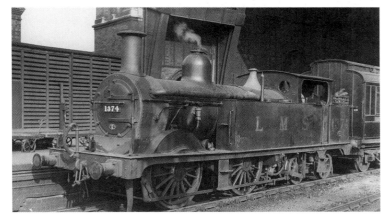

A nocturnal view of 'Jubilee' class No. 45619 *Nigeria* about to depart from St Pancras for the north.

A common sight in Liverpool Street station in the 1950s were 'Britannia' class locomotives. Here No. 70030 *William Wordsworth* is ready to move out of the smoky atmosphere.

B1 No. 61104 heads another train out of Liverpool Street.

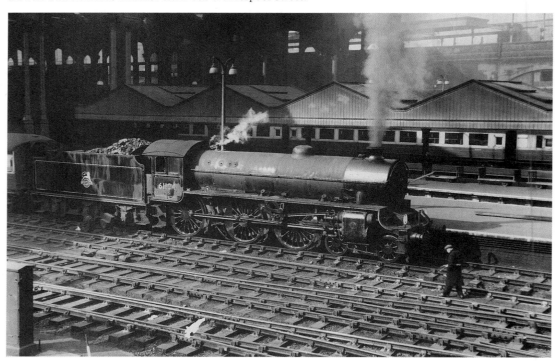

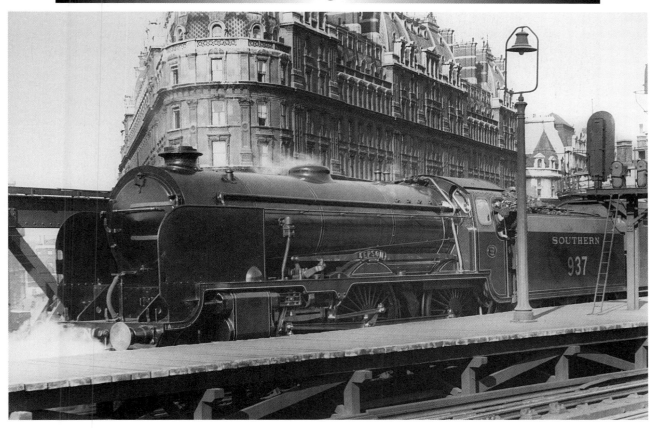

'Schools' 4–4–0 *Epsom* at Charing Cross, 1930s.

A later view of 2–6–0 No. 31908 at the same spot.

The practice of giving a train a special name goes back almost to the start of railways, not instigated by officialdom but by railway workers calling a regular train by a descriptive name. Most of the named trains in the twentieth century were the result of the companies recognising that good publicity was to be gained by giving a train a name and putting an attractive headboard on the engine.

Running along the sea wall near Teignmouth is 'The Torbay Express', hauled by No. 5008 *Raglan Castle*.

Speeding towards the Welsh capital is No. 1015 *County of Gloucester* with the 'South Wales Pullman', seen here near Stoke Gifford.

Headboard of the 'Capitals United Express',
Paddington–Cardiff.

No. 4080 *Powderham Castle* with 'The Red
Dragon' express at the top of Patchway Bank.

The 'Devon Belle' at Exeter with 'West Country' class No. 34041 *Wilton* in charge.

A representative of one of the most powerful 4–4–0 locomotives, 'Schools' class No. 30923 *Bradfield* with 'The Man of Kent'.

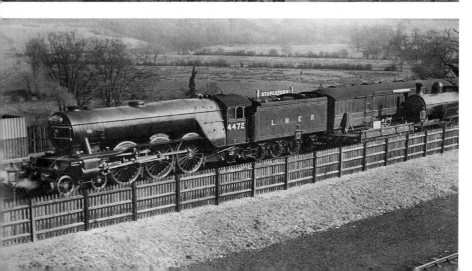

No. 4472 *Flying Scotsman* at the head of 'The Flying Scotsman', stopped at Stapleford, 1930s.

'The Royal Scot' near Stafford, with 'Coronation' class 4–6–2 No. 46240 *City of Coventry* in charge.

Above, left: Headboard of the 'Tees–Tyne Pullman', King's Cross–Newcastle.

Above, right: 'Atlantic Coast Express', Waterloo–Padstow–Bude–Ilfracombe.

Right: 'The Ulster Express', Euston–Heysham.

I wish I knew more about the Irish railway system but I have to admit I know very little. Among my archive I have some 300 negatives of steam engines from a number of Irish companies. Various people have given me information regarding these pictures. Somebody will always be able to tell where the photograph was taken or at least give an educated guess. But giving a date can be difficult. That's why I am always happy to receive further information.

Great Southern & Western Railway No. 47, a 4–4–0T.

Opposite ....

Top: Dublin & South Eastern Railway 4–4–0 *Rathnew*, built at the turn of the twentieth century.

Bottom: County Donegal Joint Railway No. 14 Walker railcar at Stranorlar, 1954.

Great Northern Railway of Ireland 4–4–0 No. 84 *Falcon*, built to work fast trains between Dublin and Belfast, 1954.

Opposite ....

Top: Great Southern Railway 0–4–0 WT No. 76.

Bottom: Great Southern Railway 0–6–4T inspection locomotive No. 92.

The Isle of Wight railway system was run by several railway companies, including the Isle of Wight Railway and the Isle of Wight Central Railway. Eventually the system was amalgamated into the SR (I of W). Freshwater is the furthest west and Bembridge the furthest east. A variety of small tank engines were used but these were replaced by Adam 4ft 10in 0–4–4T. For visitors travelling by boat to the island, Ryde Pier station was the landing point.

Approaching Brading on the Isle of Wight is No. 22 *Brading*.

High in the air. An LSWR locomotive is transferred by crane for transport by boat to the Isle of Wight.

No. 31 *Chale* receives attention, Isle of Wight.

No. 29 *Alverstone* in a rural setting, Isle of Wight.

Most of the railway system in the Isle of Man is 3ft gauge. The locomotives are all the same design, built between the 1870s and the early 1900s and painted green with a large brass dome. They are unusual in that they carry a brass number on the chimney. There is also an electric railway system, including the Manx Electric Tramway and the route from Laxey to the summit of Snaefell. Douglas also has a short railway along the promenade which is horse-drawn. There were about fifty stations on the island, Port Erin being the southernmost and Ramsey the most northerly.

Above: No. 4 *Loch* receives a final polish at Port Soderick on the Isle of Man.

Left: The brass number on the funnel of Isle of Man No. 14 *Thornhill*.

Opposite ....

Top: No. 10 *G.H. Wood* at an unidentified location on the Isle of Man.

Bottom: A peaceful summer setting for No. 12 *Hutchinson*, Isle of Man.

The Snowdon Mountain Railway opened in the 1890s to 2ft 7½in gauge and is one of the few systems that runs on a rack. A rack is a rail with teeth laid between the tracks. A gear wheel on the locomotive engages in this rack, making sure the enginemen have complete control on the steep incline. The railway had not been open very long when one of its engines was blown off the track and down a ravine. There may still be bits of the locomotive rusting in the ravine as it was never recovered.

No. 5 *Moel Siabbod*, built in 1896 in a Swiss loco works.

Opposite

Top: No. 6 *Padarn* near the top of Snowdon. The photograph clearly shows the rack between the lines.

Bottom: A pre-war view of No. 4 *Snowdon*, with a relaxed driver posing for the camera.

The Vale of Rheidol is a narrow-gauge steam railway that runs from Aberystwyth to Devil's Bridge. It had the distinction of still being steam hauled and owned by British Rail many years after the demise of steam on the main line. The 1ft 11½in gauge line has three locos. The oldest, *Prince of Wales*, was built in 1902 and Nos 7 and 8 in about 1924. The line was originally owned by the Cambrian Railway, until taken over at the grouping by the GWR.

No. 7 taking water on its way to Devil's Bridge.

Opposite ....

Top: On a wet day the fireman of *Prince of Wales* throws sand on the rails.

Bottom: No. 9 reaches its destination at Devil's Bridge.

The Somerset and Dorset line from Bath to Bournemouth via Templecombe was unkindly nicknamed the 'Slow and Dirty'. It may have been a bit on the slow side because it had to traverse the Mendip Hills. As a result it was very up and down with quite severe curves. But as for dirty, the pictures I have in my archive show very clean engines. Its closure was very controversial. Trains were timed to miss ongoing connections, giving the impression the line was unprofitable and should be closed in favour of the route to Bournemouth via Oxford.

Class 5 No. 44810 leaving Bath Green Park.

0–6–0 No. 44601 pilots a Standard Class 5 on a summer train to Bournemouth. This photograph was taken at Midford.

Sentinel No. 47191 used for shunting in the Radstock area, a Somerset coal-mining area.

A spotless S&DJR 0–6–0 No. 28 at Bournemouth West.

4–4–0 No. 45 waits to leave Bournemouth West.

No. 19 at Bournemouth West.

No. 15 at Bournemouth West.

An early view of Bath Green Park.

Another delve into the archive. I have tried this time to show some of the more unusual locomotives and some of the smaller lines. When looking through the glass negatives, it's a question of what to reject. I spend hours studying them with a magnifying glass. I can easily lose myself in the picture. Everything comes to life in my imagination. It will take a fellow enthusiast to understand.

Caledonian Railway No. 604.

The Garstang and Knott End Railway, with locomotive *Knott End* at Knott End station.

Nidd Valley Railway locomotive *Mitchell* at Scarhouse in 1923.

Could this be Captain Mainwaring driving the replica *Rocket* in 1925?

And could this be the Fat Controller coming to have a word with the photographer at King's Cross?

Probably a member of the shed staff is seen here posing with his new motorcycle (registration TB8595) in front of Midland Railway No. 449.

A Hetton Colliery locomotive at the Darlington Cavalcade, 1925.

A very early photograph of No. 1 *Gazelle* of the Shropshire and Montgomery Railway, believed to have been taken at King's Lynn in 1893 where it was built.

GWR 2–2–2 No. 160, *c.* 1900.

Weymouth Quay is the setting for this view of GWR locomotive *Hook Norton*. Judging by the clothes worn by the people in this photograph, it was probably taken in the 1920s.

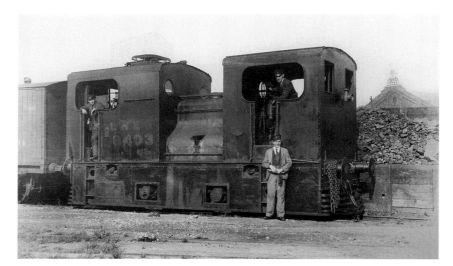

LNER No. 8403.

Lancashire &
Yorkshire Railway
2–4–0 No. 460 with
a directors'
inspection coach.

A Great Central
Railway local train
with 2–4–0T No. 24
at the head,
photographed at
Aylesbury.

The Lancashire &
Yorkshire Railway
grain store at
Fleetwood.

0–4–2 *Cleveland*,
built by Stroudley
between 1882 and
1891, heads a train
at Portsmouth
Harbour.

The 0–6–0T
narrow-gauge
locomotive *Devon*.

As an archivist and collector of original negatives it is always frustrating to have wonderful views of locomotives, trains and stations with no information. The locomotives can usually be identified but dates and locations are a different matter, so I am hoping someone may recognise the following and let me know.

1948 exchanges – Southern 'West Country' 34004 *Yeovil* in Scotland. When it was realised at the end of the Second World War that the railways were in a run-down state the government decided nationalisation was the answer. On 1 January 1948 the four railway companies became British Railways, and to find out which engines were the best a programme of exchanges took place.

Opposite

Top: A 4–4–4–4 experimental locomotive.

Bottom: London & South Western 4–6–0 No. 449 photographed at Salisbury, early 1920s.

LNWR No. 1918 *Renown*, a 'Jubilee' class Compound built in about 1900.

A Lancashire & Yorkshire Railway 2–4–2T.

0–6–0PT No. 7442.

Midland Railway 'Spinner' No. 29.

LB&SCR No. 209.

Scotland's wonderful scenery produces superb settings for photographs of steam engines.

The 'Fife Coast Express' with B1 No. 61172 at its head near Crail, 1956.

Opposite ....

Top: An unidentified industrial scene, early twentieth century.

Bottom: Cambrian Railway No. 13.

A lovely Scottish view of Arisaig, near Mallaig.

No. 60537 *Bachelor's Button* crossing the Tay Bridge, 1957.

4–4–2 No. 509 *Duke of Rothesay* and No. 421 leaving Aberdeen.

No. 60161 *North British* heads a rake of Pullmans through Prince's Street Gardens, with Edinburgh Castle in the background.

Scotland is not alone in producing lovely scenic views – Wales is also blessed with stunning locations, especially along the Cambrian route.

Dovey Junction is the setting for No. 7818 *Granville Manor* with the 'Cambrian Coast Express'.

A one-coach train approaching Port Madoc with Prairie tank 4549 on the front.

'Royal Scot' No. 6113 *Cameronian* leaving Conway Bridge.

Conway Castle, early 1900s. The train is headed by a 2–2–2.

North Wales Granite Company locomotive *Conway*.

The longest station name board in Britain.

In the 1920s steam railcars were introduced for service on branch lines where traffic was light. Most railcars were not very popular with passengers as they were noisy and subject to vibration; very few lasted beyond the mid-1940s.

LNER No. 2130 *Bang Up*, a Clayton railcar, at Stevenage, 1929.

Taff Vale Railway No. 6, built by Avonside, 1904.

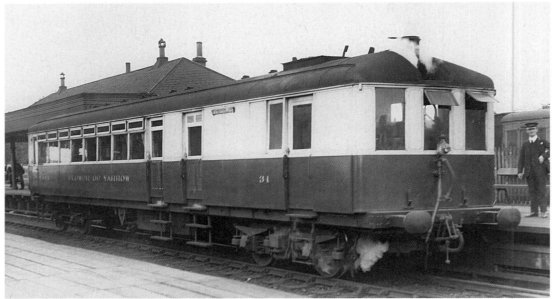

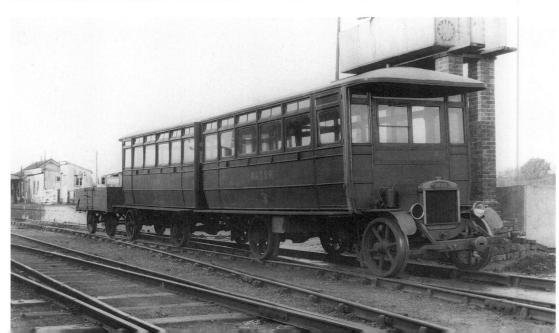

Although I am a dedicated steam enthusiast, I can still understand those who love the diesels, particularly the early varieties with their distinctive looks and sounds. I have many thousands of diesel photographs in my archive and have selected a few of the most interesting.

LMS No. 1831. Originally a Johnson 0–6–0T steam locomotive, it was rebuilt as a diesel shunter in 1932.

Opposite ....

Top: GWR No. 63. Built in 1906, it was converted to a trailer after withdrawal in 1927.

Centre: LNER No. 31 *Flower of Yarrow*, a Sentinal railcar.

Bottom: Kent & East Sussex Railway No. 3 at Rolvenden.

LMS No. 7050, 1930s.

W20, an early GWR railcar, at Shrewsbury.

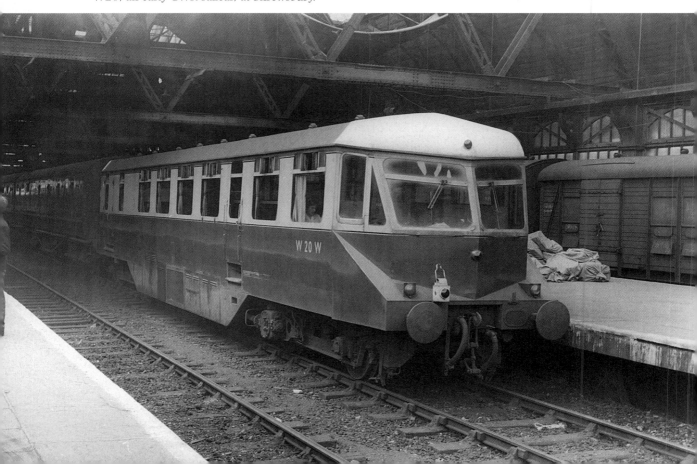

No. 18000 photographed at Swindon as part of a gas turbine experiment in the 1950s.

LMS No. 10000 at Surbiton. Built in the 1940s, this was one of a pair known as the 'twins'.

The first diesel-hydraulic built at Swindon, No. D800 *Sir Brian Robertson*, 1958.

D1005 *Western Venturer* receives a wash at Cardiff's Canton depot.

The prototype Deltic with two railwaymen making a close inspection, 1950s.

Hymek No. 7061 heads a stone train through Stoke Gifford.

We have to be grateful to Sir Billy Butlin for saving several locomotives for our enjoyment. I don't know if it was his idea or someone suggested to him that a steam locomotive placed on display at his holiday camps would be an attraction. One of these engines was No. 46229 *Duchess of Hamilton*, shown in the following photographs on display at Butlin's holiday camp at Minehead, then being towed to Swindon for restoration. It was used on many enthusiasts' railtours and there has been talk of returning it to its pre-war streamlined condition, so my final picture is of it in streamlined form leaving Shrewsbury on a running-in turn to Crewe.

The *Duchess* on the turntable at Butlin's, Minehead.

Opposite ....

Top: Another class of diesel that was popular with enthusiasts, 'Peak' No. 45025 at Cheltenham.

Bottom: Deltic No. 9006 in early colours and before naming at Haymarket.

No. 46229 in preservation heads a special near Ludlow on its way to Shrewsbury.

Opposite, below: Being towed through Blue Anchor on the way to Swindon.

Below: No. 6229 in pre-war streamlined form leaves Shrewsbury.

Photographing steam engines gave me great pleasure, and collecting negatives and starting an archive to preserve private collections after steam finished has kept my interest going. Following a family tragedy I turned to drawing and painting, being inspired by the superb works of David Shepherd. While I know I shall never achieve his level, I can recommend art as a wonderful therapeutic and relaxing activity. These four views of mine show that if you have a patient nature and need to relax, then have a go.

Rex Conway's forthcoming book is

Rex Conway's
WESTERN
STEAM JOURNEY

Published late 2007

Two 4–6–0 'Counties' on Shrewsbury shed, 1016 *County of Hants* and 1003 *County of Wilts*.